I WANT TO KNOW ABOUT
Ocean Life

by Alison Howard

NEW
FOREST
PRESS

I WANT TO KNOW ABOUT

Ocean Life

Publisher: Tim Cook   Editor: Valerie J. Weber   Designer: Matt Harding

ISBN 978 1 84898 526 1
Library of Congress Control Number: 2011924962

U.S. publication © 2011 New Forest Press
Published in arrangement with Black Rabbit Books

PO Box 784, Mankato, MN 56002

www.newforestpress.com
Printed in the USA
15 14 13 12 11 1 2 3 4 5

Picture Credits:
(t=top, b=bottom, c=center, l=left, r=right)
Alamy: 15. Shutterstock: Front cover, 1, 2, 3 (all), 5 (all), 6 (all), 8 (all), 10b, 12 (all), 13, 14b, 16 (all), 18 (all), 19, 20b, 21, 22b, 24 (all), 26 (all), 28b, back cover. Science Photo Library: 23, 25. ticktock Media Archive: 4, 7, 9, 10c, 11, 14c, 17, 20, 22c, 27, 28c, 29.

# CONTENTS

OCEAN LIFE

Words that appear in **bold** are defined in the glossary.

A World of Ocean Animals

Thousands of different kinds of animals live in the oceans. **Mammals** leap, play, and hunt in the water. Like people, they are **warm-blooded** and breathe air.

Fish swim through the oceans. They use **gills** to get **oxygen** from the water. **Scales** cover their bodies. They are vertebrates, which means they have a backbone. **Invertebrates** crawl along the ocean floor and swim through deep or shallow waters. Unlike fish, invertebrates do not have a backbone. However, some have **tentacles**, **antennae**, and hard shells.

Some sea creatures swim through all the oceans. Others live only in the waters around one country, such as Japan. When you read about an animal, see if you can find the place where it lives on the map. You can also look for the part of the world where you live.

This world map shows the continents in bold uppercase letters and countries in bold lowercase letters.

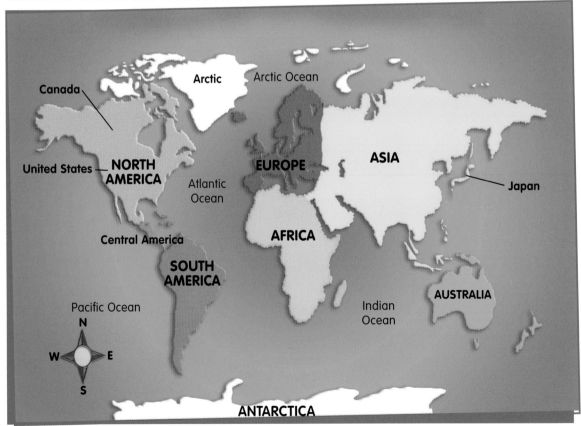

Where Do Ocean Animals Live?

Some sea animals live at the bottom of the ocean. No sunlight can reach the ocean floor. Only deep-sea **submarines** can find these creatures. Other sea animals swim just below the waves. Some can jump right out of the water or dive down deep. Others move between deep and shallow waters.

The different types of places where animals live are called habitats. Look for these pictures. They will show you what kind of habitat each animal lives in.

oceans: vast areas of water

polar regions: cold frozen places in the very north and south of the earth

seabed: the bottom of the ocean

seashore: land along the edges of oceans and seas

tropical waters: warm waters

What Do Ocean Animals Eat?

algae

fish

invertebrates

mammals

plankton

plants

Clownfish

Clownfish live in warm waters in many parts of the world. These fish hide among the stinging tentacles of anemones. **Predators** are afraid to grab the clownfish from the tentacles.

But the anemone does not hurt the clownfish. Slime on the clownfish's body protects it from the anemone's poison.

In return, the clownfish eats animals living on the anemeone's skin. It also feeds on **algae**, **plankton**, **crustaceans**, and **mollusks**.

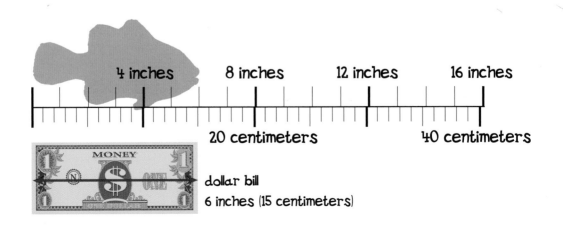

4 inches   8 inches   12 inches   16 inches

20 centimeters   40 centimeters

dollar bill
6 inches (15 centimeters)

A clownfish's bright orange and white markings look like a clown's face paint.

anemone

Coral

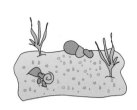 

Corals are small invertebrate animals found in oceans around the world. They come in many different colors and shapes.

A single coral is also called a polyp. A hard skeleton surrounds its tiny, soft body. Coral polyps fasten themselves to other polyps or the sea floor. Together they form large corals that often look like plants or rocks.

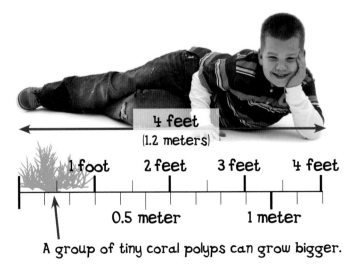

4 feet
(1.2 meters)

1 foot   2 feet   3 feet   4 feet

0.5 meter   1 meter

A group of tiny coral polyps can grow bigger.

When a polyp dies, its skeleton remains. More polyps grow and die on top of it. They form huge areas called reefs.

Corals eat plankton and tiny sea creatures. They catch their **prey** using tentacles that surround their mouths.

Great White Shark

The great white shark is the most dangerous fish in the sea. It hunts along the coasts of Asia, North America, southern Africa, Australia, and Japan.

The great white shark has powerful jaws and rows of pointed teeth. Its eyesight is sharp, and its sense of smell is keen. It can smell its prey or a tiny drop of blood from far away. It eats fish, seals, dolphins, and even small whales and other sharks.

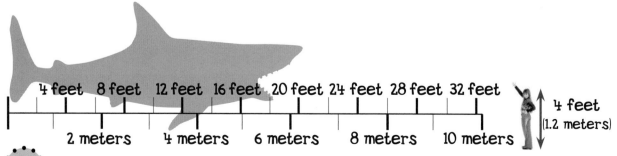

4 feet   8 feet   12 feet   16 feet   20 feet   24 feet   28 feet   32 feet

4 feet
(1.2 meters)

2 meters   4 meters   6 meters   8 meters   10 meters

A great white shark's teeth can grow to 3 inches (8 centimeters) long. If it loses a tooth, it can grow a new one.

Hermit Crab

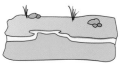

The hermit crab is found in oceans all over the world. It also lives on land and sometimes in trees!

The eyes of hermit crabs are on the end of stalks that stick out of their heads.

Hermit crabs have ten legs. The two front legs have claws.

4 inches   8 inches   12 inches   16 inches

20 centimeters   40 centimeters

dollar bill
6 inches (15 centimeters)

A hermit crab lives in shells left behind by other animals. When it grows out of its shell, it just moves to a bigger one.

Hermit crabs are **scavengers**. They eat anything they can find, including plants, plankton, and even dead sea creatures.

Jellyfish

Jellyfish live in oceans all over the world. These invertebrates have soft bodies. They sting their prey with long, **poisonous** tentacles. There are many different kinds and sizes of jellyfish.

The box jellyfish is pale blue and **transparent**. It is hard to see even in clear water. The sting of the box jellyfish is painful and deadly.

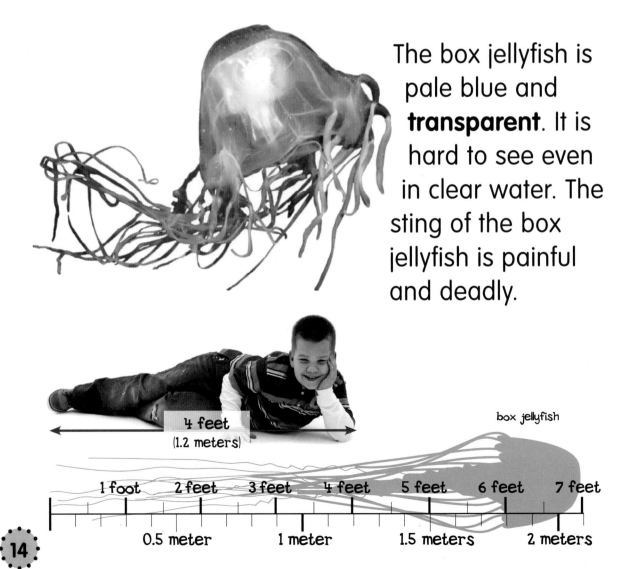

4 feet
(1.2 meters)

box jellyfish

| 1 foot | 2 feet | 3 feet | 4 feet | 5 feet | 6 feet | 7 feet |

| 0.5 meter | 1 meter | 1.5 meters | 2 meters |

cannonball jellyfish.

A jellyfish's body is shaped like an upside-down bowl. Its mouth is inside the bowl at the center.

15

Moray Eel

Moray eels live in coral reefs and shallow **coastal** waters in warm ocean areas. They back their long bodies into cracks in coral and rocks. There they hide, waiting for their prey.

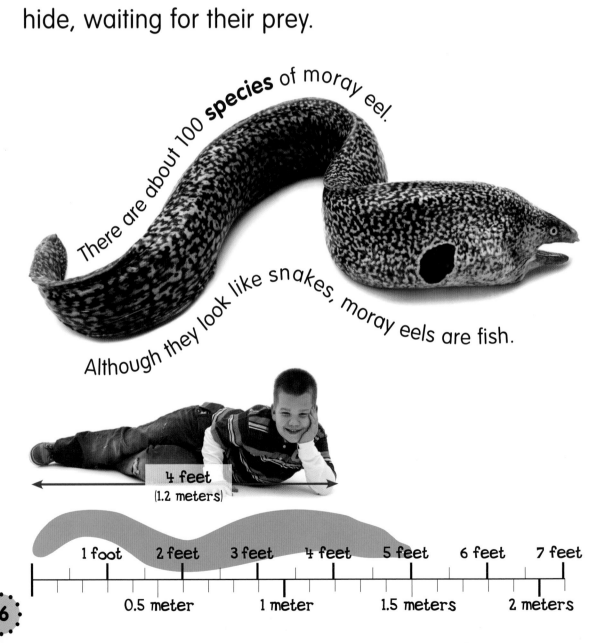

There are about 100 **species** of moray eel.

Although they look like snakes, moray eels are fish.

4 feet
(1.2 meters)

| 1 foot | 2 feet | 3 feet | 4 feet | 5 feet | 6 feet | 7 feet |

| 0.5 meter | 1 meter | 1.5 meters | 2 meters |

Sharp teeth line their wide mouths. Prey, such as fish and octopuses, have little chance of escape.

Octopus

Octopuses live all over the world, from shallow seas to deep oceans. Suckers cover their eight tentacles, or arms. They use these to catch fish and crustaceans to eat.

To escape from a predator, an octopus squirts a black, inky liquid into the water. The predators cannot see it, and the octopus can swim away.

There are 100 different species of octopuses. The largest is the giant Pacific octopus, which is 16 feet (5 meters) long.

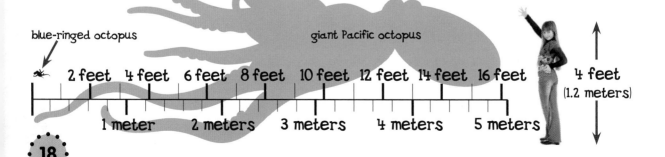

blue-ringed octopus

giant Pacific octopus

2 feet   4 feet   6 feet   8 feet   10 feet   12 feet   14 feet   16 feet

4 feet
(1.2 meters)

1 meter   2 meters   3 meters   4 meters   5 meters

The blue-ringed octopus
lives in shallow pools off
the coast of Australia.
It is one of the most
dangerous animals in the
sea. Its poisonous sting
can kill a person.

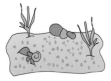

Sea Horse

Sea horses are small, bony fish. They live in warm water from North America to South America as well as near Asia and Australia. Sea horses use their tails to cling to seaweed. Their heads are shaped like horses' heads.

Sea horses swim very slowly. To hide from predators, they change their color. Then they blend in with the plants and coral around them.

The sea horse does not have scales like other fish. Instead, bony plates cover its body.

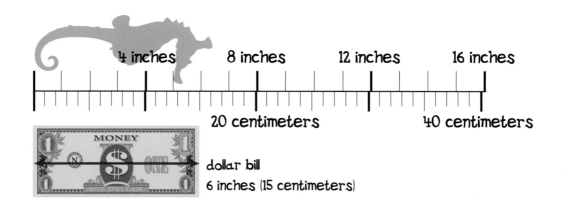

4 inches   8 inches   12 inches   16 inches

20 centimeters   40 centimeters

dollar bill
6 inches (15 centimeters)

The female puts her eggs inside the male's body. The male takes care of them until they **hatch**.

male sea horse with eggs

Sperm Whale

Sperm whales swim through the deep oceans of the world. These mammals usually travel in groups called pods. They search for squids, octopuses, and big fish to eat.

Sperm whales can dive up to 2 miles (3.2 kilometers) below the water's surface. They can stay underwater for more than an hour.

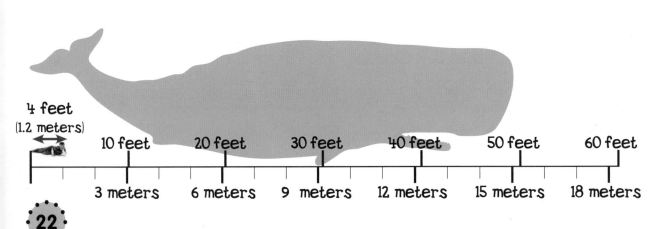

4 feet
(1.2 meters)

10 feet   20 feet   30 feet   40 feet   50 feet   60 feet

3 meters   6 meters   9 meters   12 meters   15 meters   18 meters

Whales breathe air from blowholes on top of their heads.

The sperm whale's huge head makes up one-third of its size.

Small **flippers** help steer it though the water.

Squid

Squids are **marine** mollusks that hunt from shallow seas to deep oceans. They are closely related to octopuses. Squid eat fish, crustaceans, and other squid.

Squids **communicate** with color. Muscles change the size and color of spots on their skin. The colors show that the squids are angry or scared.

Giant squid can grow to 60 feet (18 meters). Their eyes are as big as a human head!

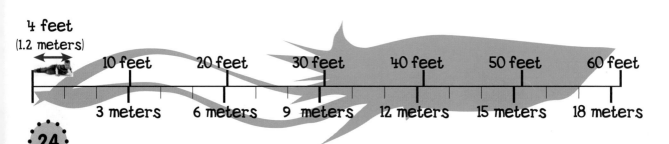

4 feet
(1.2 meters)

10 feet   20 feet   30 feet   40 feet   50 feet   60 feet

3 meters   6 meters   9 meters   12 meters   15 meters   18 meters

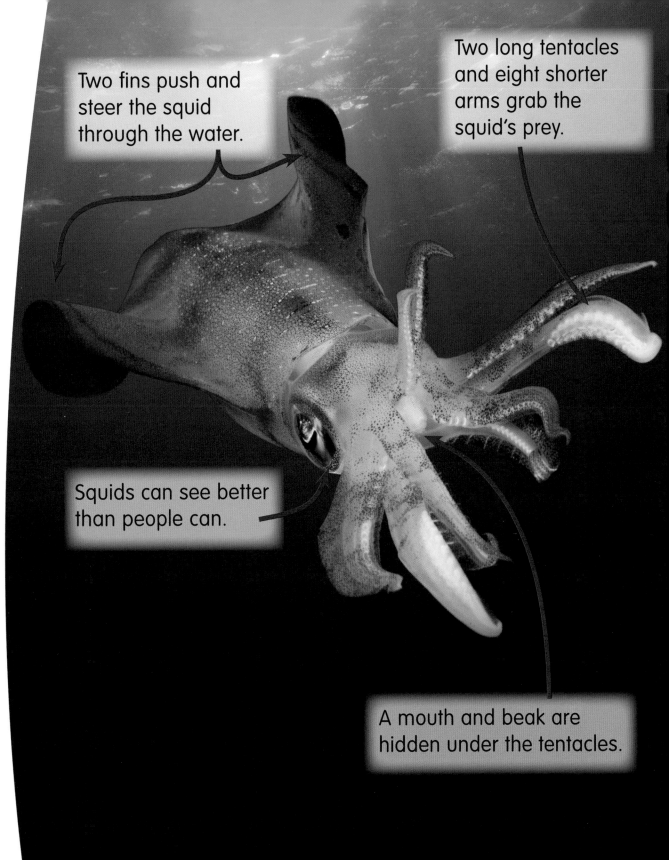

Two fins push and steer the squid through the water.

Two long tentacles and eight shorter arms grab the squid's prey.

Squids can see better than people can.

A mouth and beak are hidden under the tentacles.

25

Starfish

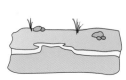

Starfish are not really fish. They are marine invertebrates. They live in shallow waters and deep seas around the world.

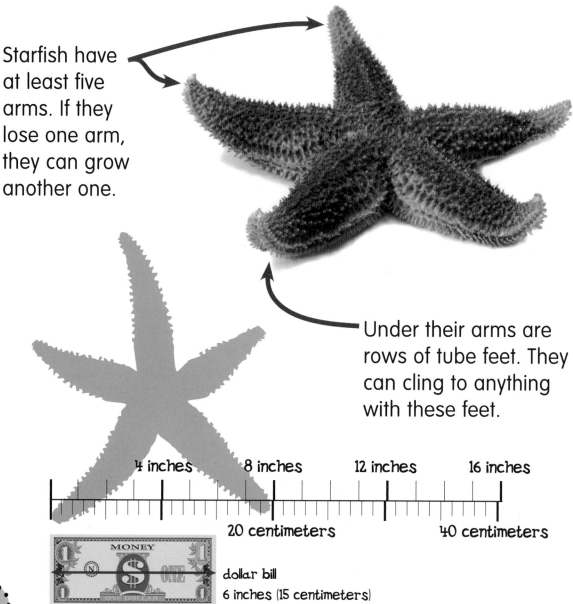

Starfish have at least five arms. If they lose one arm, they can grow another one.

Under their arms are rows of tube feet. They can cling to anything with these feet.

4 inches   8 inches   12 inches   16 inches

20 centimeters   40 centimeters

dollar bill
6 inches (15 centimeters)

A starfish can push its stomach out from its body. The stomach covers the starfish's prey and **digests** it.

Walrus

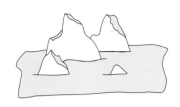

Walruses live in the Arctic. They hunt for **shellfish** and fish in the sea. These huge mammals can stay underwater for twenty-five minutes. They haul themselves onto land to rest.

A baby walrus is called a calf. This big baby weighed about 165 pounds (75 kilograms) when it was born!

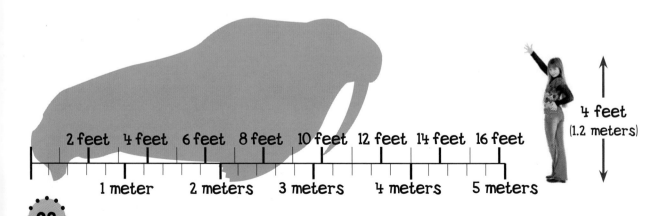

2 feet   4 feet   6 feet   8 feet   10 feet   12 feet   14 feet   16 feet

1 meter   2 meters   3 meters   4 meters   5 meters

4 feet
(1.2 meters)

An adult male's **tusks** can grow to over 3 feet (1 meter) long.

Walruses have thick, wrinkled skin.

Walruses use their flippers and sometimes their tusks to crawl on land. Hundreds of walruses often lie together on beaches or chunks of floating ice.

For More Information

Books to Read

Berkes, Marianne. *Over in the Ocean: In a Coral Reef.* Dawn Publications

Gross, Miriam J. *The Moray Eel.* Rosen Publishing Group's PowerKids Press

Marsh, Laura. *Whales.* National Geographic

Weber, Valerie. *Walruses.* Weekly Reader Science

Zollman, Pam. *A Shark Pup Grows Up.* Children's Press

Places to Explore

Florida Aquarium
701 Channelside Drive
Tampa, FL 33602
www.flaquarium.org
Get to know five different sharks from around the world, watch clownfish, octopuses, and other marine life swim, and then splash around this aquarium's water park.

Monterey Bay Aquarium
886 Cannery Row
Monterey, CA 93940
www.montereybayaquarium.org
Dive into a day of exploration and watch ocean life, from jellyfish to zebra moray eels, glide before your eyes.

New York Aquarium
Surf Avenue & West 8th Street
Brooklyn, NY 11224.
www.nyaquarium.com
Peer deeply into coral reefs and watch trainers feed walruses and other ocean life.

Shedd Aquarium
1200 South Lake Shore Drive
Chicago, IL 60605
www.sheddaquarium.org
Get face-to-face with a dolphin, meet Nunavik the baby beluga whale, and stroll past a million more ocean-life creatures in this amazing aquarium.

Web Sites to Visit

kids.nationalgeographic.com/kids/animals/ creaturefeature/pufferfish
Dive into puffer fish facts and photos. See how a puffer fish can make an otter go away. Then click on the map to see where in the world puffer fish live. You can also find other ocean animals here.

nationalzoo.si.edu/Animals/OceanLiving/ ForKids/default.cfm
Figure out the difference between seals and sea lions, solve an online jigsaw puzzle, and learn more about ocean life.

www.kidport.com/reflib/science/Videos/ Animals/Echinoderms/Starfish.htm
Watch starfish swim, see their tube feet in action, and learn about their feeding habits.

www.primarygames.com/science/ocean/ games.htm
Play games with ocean themes and watch a video of a manatee.

Publisher's note: We have reviewed these Web sites to ensure that they are suitable for children. Web sites change frequently, however, so children should be closely supervised whenever they access the Internet.

Glossary

algae — a group of simple plants, such as seaweed, without flowers

antennae — long thin feelers on the heads of some ocean animals and insects

coastal — describes the edge of the land near the sea

communicate — to pass along information or feelings

crustaceans — animals with hard shells that usually live in water

digests — breaks down food so it can be used by the body for energy

flippers — broad flat limbs, like arms, on a whale or other ocean animal. Animals use flippers to swim and to move on land.

gills — parts of an animal's body used for taking in oxygen underwater

hatch — to break out of an egg

invertebrates — animals without backbones

mammals — animals that breathe air with their lungs, make their own body heat, produce milk for their babies, and have fur

marine — having to do with or living in the sea

mollusks — animals with soft bodies and no backbones. Most mollusks have shells to protect their bodies.

oxygen — a gas that has no smell or color. People, animals, and plants need oxygen to live.

plankton — tiny plants and animals that float in the sea. Many sea animals eat plankton.

poisonous — describing something that can kill or hurt an animal or a person

predators — animals that hunt other animals for food

prey — animals that are hunted for food

scales — small stiff plates on the bodies of animals such as fish, lizards, and snakes

scavengers — animals that eat creatures that are already dead instead of killing live ones

shellfish — an animal that lives in water and is protected by a shell

species — a group of living things of the same type

submarines — ships that can travel underwater

tentacles — long thin growths on octopuses, squids, jellyfish, and other animals. Tentacles are used to hold, feel, and move.

transparent — allowing light to pass through so that something on the other side can be seen

tusks — long, pointed teeth that grow out of an animal's face or mouth

warm-blooded — able to produce body heat. Animals that are warm-blooded usually stay the same temperature.

Index